From a Nobody...
...To a Somebody

by Valerie Humphreys

This edition published in Great Britain 2020 by

Farthings Publishing,
2G Montrosa,
Esplanade Road,
Scarborough YO11 2AX

http://www.farthings-publishing.com
dgfowler@gmail.com

ISBN 978-1-716-67006-0

September 2020 (g)

Contents

Acknowledgements

Without the help and financial support of so many people I would never have been able to help Denis achieve his desired wish to become a doctor.

My two daughters, Katharine and Jane, my Sons in law and my four older grandchildren have given endless practical help at all of the Strawberry and Cream tea events and Lunches.

Many people over the years have given Raffle Prizes and close friends Rosemary and Pat have sold raffle tickets at each event. I appreciate all the neighbours and friends who have made and given delicious desserts for my luncheons.

Many colleagues who I swim with and also members of the RNLI, Scalby Wives Club, Sightsavers International Committee, the Business and Professional Womens Clubs, and St Mark's Church, Newby, have all supported generously. I cannot name all these people here. However, I must name a few who have given me constant encouragement and support. Barbara and Allan Mutter, Nahar Mamoon, Hazel Jackson, Doreen Brooke and Gordon Pottage. Not forgetting Marialuz Moreno Badia who lives in the USA and who I met while waiting in Rwanda at Kigali airport. She really encouraged me to write this book.

To David Fowler, semi-retired he told me, of Farthings Publishing who graciously said he would proof read and publish my book.

My grateful thanks to each and every one of you.

Every penny made from the sale of this book will go towards buying further desperately needed medical equipment for the Victorious Medical Centre, which is situated in a very impoverished area of SW Uganda. Denis is now the Director/ Resident Doctor and Surgeon in charge.

INTRODUCTION

Shoebills and Gorillas

My younger sister Anita asked if I would like to go on a birding holiday with her. She had already visited several African countries. On a weekend stay at her home I was looking through The Travelling Naturalist holiday brochure and came across a full page with a picture of a family of gorillas. I exclaimed, "Anita I can't see birds high up in the trees, but I could see gorillas." This was in Uganda and she replied, "Well we will go there then!" We booked the holiday the next day.

The two of us set off on our journey to Uganda on 19th January 2010 to see the wildlife. On our arrival at Entebbe airport we were joined by the rest of our party, 11 people in all plus our two guides.

At the start of our holiday we went in search of one of the worlds most desired birds, a Shoebill. We set off by getting onto a small wooden boat and moving through a maze of papyrus channels. We eventually spotted our quarry and gently glided towards it. It stood unmoving and stared at us with its cold reptile eyes. It became accustomed to our presence and spread its feathers in the sun and showed off its clog like bill.

It was all so exciting! We didn't mind too much when a huge deluge of rain came down on us and stopped us in our tracks for almost ½ hour. As well as the shoebill we saw 338 other species of bird in the country as well as an abundance of spectacular butterflies, about 30 species in all. We also saw lots of species of monkeys, baboons and chimpanzees.

But the highlight for me was the gorillas!

I visited the Impenetrable Forest at Bwindi to track and see the Rusheguru family of 19 Gorillas, from tiny babies to huge silverback.

Little did I know then that this adventure would change my life forever.

CHAPTER 1

Tracking Gorillas and a chance meeting

Our tour guides had told us on our journey to Bwindi that if we decided we could hire a porter who would assist with carrying our bag on the steep and rough terrain. The bag would have our raincoat and packed lunch in it.

My porter was a young man named Denis, hearing that name brought a shiver down my spine. I told him I would not forget his name in a hurry. My late husband's name was Dennis and he had died age just 28 of Leukaemia, leaving me at 6 months pregnant with a daughter who I called Katharine.   At that time, I had no idea that so many Ugandans are given British Christian names.

Denis helped me on the difficult climb into the forest to view the gorillas. Being in their presence must count as one of the most exciting hours of my life!! During the approach to the climb Denis and I chatted away happily asking each other about our very different lives. I found him to have a very enquiring mind which interested me. He asked if we had telephones in our country and later asked if we had "emals". After 3 attempts I realized he meant emails.

He had been working during his school holidays for pennies to make a little money to put towards his senior education. He told me, that he had a great desire someday to come to England. I said he was to study hard, get a good career and then someday he may be able to do so. I told him that for many, many years I had to work extremely hard and it was only now that I could go on such a holiday.

After walking along the approach, we started to climb up into the forest. At this point Denis wanted to assist me and asked to hold my hand. I politely declined saying I would ask if I needed help. He explained that he must hold my hand to help me. Soon the climb became much steeper with the branches and thorns reaching around us, then I certainly needed his helping hand, by pulling me up, with another porter pushing me up from behind. My travelling companions and I were allowed in the presence of the gorillas for exactly 1 hour. Then a whistle was blown, and the gorillas seemed to know what that meant, and they started to wander off on their own.

Whilst walking along the track I had noticed that Denis was wearing laced up boots, but the laces were not even fastened while all the other trackers and porters seemed to be wearing wellington boots.

At one point we had to cross a small but flowing stream and to make sure that my feet did not get wet Denis stood in the water with his feet submerged and held my hands so that I could balance on the rocks sticking out of the water.

I realized then that for the rest of our journey his boots must have been full of water.

It was some years later when I asked him why he had been wearing those boots. He explained that he was poor and did not possess a pair of wellingtons or suitable footwear, so he had been given the boots to wear and they did not fit.

After we returned from a most memorable few hours of my life- seeing the family of 19 gorillas, I paid him the Porters fee of £9.50 and gave him a tip. I handed him my business card which I had carried in my rucksack in case of loss.

About three weeks after we arrived back home, I was very surprised one day to receive a short e mail from Denis asking if I had arrived home safely. This was the beginning of our very long and interesting correspondence with each other. Here are the first three of our letters to each other.

Subject: Greetings

Hi mrs Valerie,This is denis from bwindi who travelled with you on tracking gorillas of rushegura group in Bwindi impenetrable national park.

How is your sister anitar

I wish to know whether you arrived home safely,as wise greetings from Brothers and my sister

Hope to heare from you soon.
YOURS MUSAASIZI DENIS
FROM BWINDI.

Date: Monday, February 8, 2010, 9:11 PM

Hello Denis

I was delighted to receive your e.mail and yes I arrived home safely after a very long journey. We had snow here in England when we arrived back, extremely cold!!!!!

What a wonderful time we all had while in your beautiful country, and tracking to see the Gorillas was a real highlight. Without your help and that of your friends we would have found it very difficult to achieve. I will send you some picturers when I get them sorted out.

Have you had the chance to do any more Portering since you helped me, I hope so, spend the money wisely. Work hard at your studies and I hope one day you will have a good job. Then you will be able to save and see other parts of the world.

I had to work very hard for many many years before I could have a proper holiday, but I am having my rewards now.

I will look forward to hearing from you again, tell me what you do when you are not helping people to see the Gorillas.

Kindest regards   Valerie

From: Musaasizi Denis
Sent: 11 February 2010 09:50
To: Valerie Humphreys
Subject: RE: Greetings

Hi Valerie,i first thank God that helpet you reach home safely through all parts you traveld. concerning with doing any porteing,i did not do any more because our U.C.E.Resuilts were released and started arranging for schooling.As i had told you that i wish becoming Adoctor in future,iam happy that i managed toget first grade in Uganda National ExaminationsBoard which could allow me to join any Medical course but i found my parents an able to suport me financialy they are telling me they dont have money to pus hme ahead me .so iam still at home puting my ayes on my parents.if ihappen to get money iwill inform you where i went for studies.
    as wise thank you for informing me that you are safe
 Hope to heare from yousoon.
 YOURS;MUSAASIZI DENIS.

With 3 trackers and Denis my Porter. My first picture of him.

CHAPTER 2

About Denis

The Ugandan government only pay for junior schooling not senior. Denis went to a senior school with the little money he had saved but had to leave after 3 weeks and 4 days as his money had run out and the headmaster sent him home. His father told him he must exit education. It was at this point I wanted to try to find a way of helping him.

Denis is from a family of ten children who live in an impoverished part of Uganda. He has six older brothers, all given biblical names; Obed, Moses, Ephrem, Onesmus, Jerimiah and Isiah, then number 7 was given an English name Denis. Why? It is said that number 7 in a family is the lucky one. Then came the only daughter Moreen, next Labour and last of all, Chrispus.

After a long search on Google and getting no help from the well-known National charities who I thought helped in the 3rd world countries, I discovered a Cornwall based charity called ACE (Aid Conservation Through Education) who work in the south western corner of Uganda.
I had a conversation with its founder/chairman Angela Peake, who on her first journey to Uganda had gone to see the gorillas.

Angela at that time was a junior schoolteacher and asked if she could visit a school while in the area. She was appalled by what she saw. The school she visited was built of sticks and mud and had tin sheets on the roof, but no windows, and just mud floors. No desks or chairs either for the children.

Once back home in Cornwall Angela started doing car boot sales to raise a little money for this school. She became so inspired that she and 6 of her friends became trustees and were later given charity status, and ACE was established. Sometime later, ACE supported 7 schools in the communities bordering the national parks around Kisoro.

CHAPTER 3

Sponsorship

Through Angela and the school headteachers and Inspectors in Kisoro and Bwindi Denis was checked out and was indeed very genuine. He did come from a very poverty-stricken family and all his exam results were genuine too. Although he had never attended one of the ACE schools, they said they would accept him on their sponsorship scheme IF I would become his sponsor. Until that time, I had not given any thoughts about sponsoring Denis myself, I was just looking for a way he may continue his education.

However, for over 4 months we had been corresponding with each other and I had built up a trusting and happy relationship with him. I considered that I had paid £350 for one day just to be able to see gorillas on my holiday and it was only going to cost £360 inclusive per year to give this 18-year-old young man a full year's education. My decision was made, and I let Angela know. I then wrote to Denis and told him that he had been accepted by Dan, the Director of Vision boarding school in Kisoro. Lastly, I was able to tell him that his Sponsor would be me.!!

Now he would have to prove to me that my gut feelings that he was a genuine, intelligent and caring young man when I met him for such a short time in the Impenetrable forest, were indeed true.!! I told him that I was about to invest a lot of money in his senior education, in the hopes that he would become a high achiever. I added that he would have the opportunity to work hard for both himself and for me and that I realised that not many young people in his country are given the chance he was being offered.

The school the sponsored children attend as boarders is VISION senior school in Kisoro a 6 ½ hour journey from Bwindi near Denis's home. At first Angela doubted this unknown young man would be prepared to travel all that distance to a strange school in a strange area. However, Denis took it in his stride as nothing was going to stop him from continuing with his senior education.

At no time then was any money ever sent directly to Denis. I forwarded the fees needed to ACE in Cornwall and they in turn sent it out to Uganda and paid Vision school. After all the formalities to get him a place at this school, Denis set off on his long journey. He travelled overnight from his home and with several changes of transport he arrived in Kisoro in the early morning on May 23rd, 2010. He was met at the bus stop by the local school inspector William.

Before being taken to the Vision school Denis requested to go to an internet cafe so he could send me and Angela an email telling us he had arrived. After only 10 days at Vision school I received a message through ACE telling me that the headmaster and all the teaching staff who had met Denis, were very impressed and had great hopes of him to achieve very highly.

This of course gave me pleasure and confidence that I had met someone rather special and worthy of my support!

CHAPTER 4

Support for, and meeting Denis again

It had taken four months to get all the information needed to make sure Denis was genuine. Consequently, he had missed six months of his senior five studies.

During each of the three terms of the year each sponsored child must write a letter to their sponsor, usually a few short lines. However, from Denis I received a wonderful long letter giving me all the details of his short time at the Vision school.

Scans of the original handwritten letter, a typed version of which appears on the next page.

He had worked extra hard to enable himself to catch up with the other students in that year.

During the Christmas holidays he travelled back home to Bwindi and studied hard day and night with only a paraffin lamp, there being no electricity or running water in the village where his home is.

By the time he returned to Vision school to start in senior six year he had caught up with his fellow students. Quite an achievement!

Denis, aged 18, his dormitory behind him at VISION School

We exchanged letters, some of which appear in this book, although Denis supplied a typed copy of his handwritten letter which appears on page 21 and which would not have reproduced well.

This typed copy follows on the next page:

30th July 2010

Dear sponsor.

      I first and foremost thank you very much for the support you are giving towards my education which is prospering because of you like providing for me with school fees,scholastic
materials, uniform and many others including transport.

      I wish to asure you that I got to school successfully and started serious studies and revision. I made now friends and actually helped me much in adopting to the conditions at school.

      In s.5 science class we are 15 students having BCG/A and we make extensive discussions after preps such that I can catch up with them because they had left me especially in biology and Agriculture but I tried my level best to copy biology and I am now left with few notes of Agriculture because here no time to rest, all the time is schedulled for a certain activity and I hope these holidays, I will finish copying all the notes and match on the same line with others.

      At school we get morning porriadge at 6:30 am, then at 7:00 am lessons begin, at 1:00pm we get lunch and at 2:00pm after lunch lessions begin and end at 5:30 pm .From there,we are given 1 hour to bathe and prepare for supper and night prep.Supper is at 6:30pm and at 7:00pm, night prep begins and ends at 4:30pm but for me I extend up to midnight because I like studies so much.Morning winter starts at 4:15am and at 6:30am we go for morning porriadge as the process continues.

      We have a very good playground but due to the fact that I lack enough time,I go there when relaxing my mindsor when we have interschool competition and I pray number 8 (striker). We have enough domitories each one being shared by only 6 students, we have electricity which anables us to conceterate all the time, latrines and good water is also available at school

      We have now gone back home for holidays and in these holidays, I expect to do maximum revision,copy all the notes in oder for my education to be succesful because I like studies very and very much.

      I wish you the best in whatever you are doing:
I wish you could come back to Uganda and kanungu/kisoro and see you again.Gorrillas are very happy and they also wish that you could again come to see them.
Nice time throughout your life activities.

Yours Faithfully

   MUSASIZI DENIS

CHAPTER 5

Uganda for 3 weeks - 2011

Angela had informed me that she and Vic her husband were going again to Uganda in September/October 2011 for three weeks to visit all the seven ACE schools and to visit VISION where all the ACE sponsored children were boarding and of course my boy Denis. Angela invited me to go along with them. I accepted. It so happened that my daughter Katharine and her family plus myself had booked a holiday in Newquay, Cornwall in the August of 2011 and on hearing of this Angela invited us to meet all the 7 trustees of ACE at her home.

We spent a very happy afternoon in their company in glorious sunshine while sitting in the most beautiful garden, eating a delicious Cornish cream tea. I immediately felt at ease with Angela and Vic and knew we would get along well together in Uganda.

In September 2011 I set off once more from Scarborough on my own to make the journey to Entebbe, Uganda.

I was to meet Angela and her husband Vic. They were to arrive the following morning, so a single room had been booked for me in a B & B by David Epido who is the Ugandan working there for ACE. I arrived at Entebbe airport around 10pm alone and rather nervous to be met by a Ugandan man who I had never seen before. David was standing there with a large piece of paper in his hands displaying, VALERIE HUMPHREYS.

After greetings (and in the darkest of nights), I was driven for about half an hour and eventually along a very rocky and bumpy unmade road to my B&B which seemed to be in the middle of nowhere.!!! A single room had been booked for me by David. After bringing in all my luggage David left, and I felt very alone in this strange country.
I was asked what I would like for my breakfast for the following morning. I knew they did not serve cornflakes or any cereals in Uganda, so I decided to order a poached egg on toast, I then retired to my room.

On moving my suitcase to open it for my nightclothes and toilet bag a huge COCKROACH "galloped" from under it and disappeared under my smaller case. Startled I leapt onto my bed putting my feet up well off the floor. Seeing the funny side of the situation I sent a text to my daughter in the UK telling her I had arrived safely and adding that I had seen my first wild animal in Uganda, a cockroach!

Thankfully I never saw it again.

At 7.30 the next morning I went into the dining room expecting to be served a poached egg on toast, however I was given some dry bread, no toast in Uganda in 2011 and the funniest cooked egg I have ever seen, it was flat and had been mixed white with the yoke and was brown and warm.

Around 8.30 am David had met and collected Angela and Vic at the airport and together they came to pick me up. We had all been allowed by the airline to carry extra luggage as we were working for a charity and we really struggled to get it all into our 5-seater car. As well as packing the boot to capacity we had cases between us on the back seat and on the floor in the front and around our feet!

After changing all our English money into Ugandan shillings (a much better rate in the capital city) we set off on our very long journey to Kisoro, approximately 350 miles. We arrived around 8pm at the Countryside guest house where our rooms had been booked.

On the Saturday we went for a very pleasant walk around Kisoro town and took in the beautiful hillside scenery. Then a relaxing time in the gardens of the Travellers Rest 5* hotel where we enjoyed cool fruit drinks.

Later that day Angela had arranged for us to meet the headmasters and deputy head teachers from all the seven ACE schools along with William the area school inspector, Dan the owner/director of the private Vision school and Mandela the driver of the transport for the local education authority. Following the meeting a hot meal of chicken, potatoes, gizzard (a special for guests) and greens was served. By this time, it was pouring with rain and extremely cold, because although we were under cover there were no sides to the building.

When the three of us arrived back at our Guest house of course there was no heating, so we all put on extra clothing, camisole, fleece with our raincoat on the top to keep us warm.

At home of course we would have just turned on a fan heater, but after all we were in Uganda!!!! Sunday was a day when we all just relaxed.

On the Monday morning we visited the first of the Ace supported schools called Rukongi. Here I was to see just how very thoroughly Angela inspected each of the ACE schools, both inside and out.

Inside, the floors, walls, black boards, desks (or lack of them), were in a terrible condition as were the books. The pupils had to carry their books home each day whatever the weather.

Outside, the Latrines, water tanks, play areas or lack of them, each were considered and inspected.

I could hardly wait for the afternoon!! I was so excited but very nervous as Angela, Vic and I were going to Vision School where I would meet Denis again after a 1½ years absence.

Would I recognise him?

We were taken into the Director Dan's office for greetings. Suddenly there was a young man at the door and the headmaster exclaimed "Oh Denis do come in !!" Of course, then I knew it was My Denis and we greeted each other with a hug.

By the time of this visit to Vision, Denis had already been chosen as the leader of all 37 ACE students. He went off and gathered them all into a classroom so that Angela could address them and hand out letters and gifts to each child, which had been sent by their sponsors. After this special meeting Denis and I went out into the play area to chat alone with each other. Conversation flowed easily between us. I asked if he could show me his accommodation and I was appalled when taken into a small dark room where there were three sets of bunk beds. One for each of the 6 boys to call their own. Their personal belongings had to fit on their bed.

Before I had left England, arrangements were made for Mandela to be my personal driver while using a 4x4 truck transport provided by the Kisoro Education Department for the day. This was to enable Denis to take me and Dan the director, on the long journey to visit Denis's parents and family near Bwindi. This was approximately a 5 1/2 hours journey and the same back to Kisoro later that day.

At one point on our long journey to Bwindi the vehicle stopped, and Denis got out and left. I asked where he had gone and was politely told he had gone for a comfort stop! I uttered that I could do with one too. Shortly after Mandela stopped the vehicle for me to go off into the bushes, for my comfort stop, only there were no bushes!

Leaving the 3 males in the 4x4 I walked away around a bend in the road and out of their view.

I was squatting and in mid flow when suddenly from nowhere came a motorbike carrying two people and it passed slowly by. So, what could I do, I carried on and gave them a wave!! I could not believe it for we had travelled for hours and nothing had passed us in either direction. This incident caused much laughter when I returned to our vehicle and told the three men my actions.

As we neared Denis's home area I asked if I could be shown the Bwindi hospital as that was where Denis had to walk to whenever he needed to send me an e-mail.

Along the way the vehicle would suddenly stop and one of Denis's brothers would be at my window to be introduced to me. This happened three times, I'm not quite sure which three they were, and each one would say I will see you later at the parents' home. At Bwindi hospital I was welcomed and shown all around the building. In a separate area there was a small unit where the computers were housed for the public to use and this was where Denis walked to from his home to send me his e-mails and then walk back home, a round trip of approx. 7 miles.

After greetings with his parents, who cannot speak any English, I was introduced to his 8 brothers and only sister Moreen. We then entered their tiny living room made with sticks, dung and clay where a traditional Ugandan meal was served. Matoke, beans, spinach, millet and groundnut sauce and especially killed in my honour, was chicken and a goat stew. Meat is usually only eaten on very special occasions!

In Denis's tiny home.

I only realized long after our visit that all female members of the family eat outside sitting on reed mats on the ground while the males sit inside on chairs and put their food into a bowl from larger serving dishes set on a small low table. In the impoverished areas of Uganda the people use their fingers to put their food into their mouths so before every meal a bowl with a tablet of poor-quality soap in it was offered to each person and a jug with warm water was poured over their hands. The same ritual is offered at the end of each meal. Fortunately, I was given a fork to eat with. Prayers were said by a member of the family before eating began. Later I handed out small gifts for the family and took many photographs of inside and outside the property.

With parents and siblings

On our return journey to Kisoro I asked Dan if I could meet with Denis again the following day, a Sunday. We met at 3 pm and spent the time taking tea in the garden of a beautiful hotel, Travellers Rest. We found it very easy to talk to each other for the next 3 ½ hours. It was here that I felt our personal bond had deepened.

The remainder of our time in Kisoro was taken up by visiting the seven schools which were being supported and improved by ACE. When we arrived at one of the schools, we found no teachers there at all. The children had been left playing in the playground, each with a reading book in their hand. This school later lost all support from ACE

Earlier Angela had complained after seeing that the reading books at some of the schools were still very new and told the teachers to let their children have a book to take home to read which they did. Two more schools however were taken on as many pupils were leaving Ugandan Government schools to go to an ACE school as they were much improved with new classrooms, good latrines and water tanks and excellent teachers.

This visit had been a wonderful experience for me, not an organised tour, but seeing real life in an underprivileged area of Uganda.

I arrived back home realising just how fortunate we all are in the United Kingdom.

CHAPTER 6

The long wait

During October 2011 Denis sat his Senior 6 examinations after which he returned home to await the results which would not be released until Feb/March 2012. In this time of waiting he did not stay idle. For several weeks, he took a job carrying volcanic boulders from the hillside and put them into lorries which took them to be used as foundations for buildings. Then at my suggestion he went to a local medical clinic and volunteered to work there to see if he really wanted to take up a career in medicine.

He thoroughly enjoyed his time there. Waiting for his results to be released he asked me if I would support him on a two month Introductory course on Computers, whilst waiting for the exam results. The course was at the Bwindi Amagera Training Centre and of course he successfully completed it.

In February 2012 the S6 exam results were released and Denis had scored a total of 14 points. This was enough to qualify for enrolment at a University. However, it wasn't quite enough for him to be funded by the government for a University place.

For guidance I wrote a personal letter to Dan the Director of Vision for advice on what or where Denis should attend next to continue his education. This is Dan's reply :-

From: Mbabazi Dan
Sent: 22 March 2012 17:55
To: valhumphreys@hotmail.co.uk
Subject: Denis studies

Dear Val.
It is a pleasure to communicate to you at this time.
Frankly it would be so unwise to send Denis for a certificate. Here, certificates are for those who completed Primary Seven and Senior four only. OR a person adding on the already acquired qualification. We should be thinking of a Diploma and Degree only.

With Denis' scores' scores, we encourage him to go for a Medical course, whether at degree or diploma level. For Diploma, we are waiting to see him given direct admission or for a much more marketable course, still it would be for self sponsorship. On Degree, it is self sponsorship with other costs catered for by the student himself.

Considering his performance, he can manage a degree course. He can still achieve so well. I trust him. He is not a luxurious person which makes people fail. Hope I have responded to your questions.

Greetings from my family, Vision and Myself. Extend my greetings to Angela etc

Dan

Having paid Denis's fees and living expenses for his S5 and S6 education, he had certainly worked so hard and achieved very high marks even though he has missed 6 months of his S5 year. I felt that I could not just stop helping him at this point in time. I told him to start applying to get into a University for a medical degree. It took some considerable time, in fact four months for the process to be completed. There is no postal service in Uganda, so it was difficult to access all the information.

On the 17th June 2012 Denis was admitted to Kampala International University on a 5 ½ years course of study and was to start on the 20th September 2012 as a privately sponsored student. On completion of this course he would be awarded Bachelor of Medicine and Bachelor of Surgery qualifications. However, it was not until 4th July that he finally had the admission forms in his hands!

It was at this time that I realized that this young man had to have a bank account. He had never had to handle money in his life before.

My money for his education at Vision had all been sent and paid to the school directly by ACE. Once a student has left Vision their sponsorship through ACE comes to an end. Thankfully for me Angela had agreed to handle, through ACE the money to set up Denis for his first semester in Ishaka at the Kampala International University.

By this time there were no rooms left to rent on Campus, so he needed money to rent a room off campus and buy a bed, chair, table, mosquito net and bedding etc for this tiny room, as well as fees, travel and living expenses for the first 6 months. I gave instructions to Denis to go to the bank of his choice and set up a bank account with the £50 extra I had sent him. After his first semester I was able to send his money via Money Gram or Western Union. He was then able to collect it within minutes and deposit it into his bank account.

On the 18th September 2012 at 4am Denis left his home village to make the long journey using both motorbike, taxi, and then buses to reach Ishaka at 1.35pm. An arduous trip of 9 hours 35 mins.

After settling in his very small room, he went to register with the Kampala International University (KIU) on the 20th September.

CHAPTER 7

Kampala International University

It was here in Ishaka at university that Denis discovered most of the students were from different countries like Kenya, Tanzania, Nigeria, Sudan, Somalia, Rwanda and Democratic Republic of Congo. The one thing that really shocked him was that there were only 4 Ugandan students taking Bachelor of Medicine and Surgery out of a total of 95. This was mainly because it would be far too expensive for Ugandans to study there.

To make his money go further Denis decided to cook all his meals for himself in his room as eating out was far too costly. He did all this on his bedroom floor on a small paraffin stove. At one time a friend of mine called Gordon gave me £50 to send to Denis for him to spend on himself. I was surprised and impressed when he sent me a picture of a gas cylinder he had decided to buy, to cook his food on, rather than spend it on clothes.

During the next two years he grasped every opportunity and worked extremely hard and achieved very high marks in all his examinations. He was in the top three places at the end of every semester. On every Outreach programme he was always chosen as the leader. Denis and I corresponded most weekends on the internet with e-mails, during this time.

In September 2014 I again travelled to Uganda with Angela and Vic to spend 3 weeks with them visiting schools as well as Denis. As well as visiting the 9 ACE schools in the mountainous areas around Kisoro, we also went to Vision school again where the Ace sponsored students boarded and studied.

After hearing about me sponsoring a boy in Uganda and the satisfaction and great joy it was giving me, two of my friends from Scarborough were now also sponsors of children from ACE schools. I was able to take and hand over personal gifts to each of them from their sponsor.

I also took photos of these students to give to their sponsor on my return home.

One day we were visiting a school which is on the border of the Democratic Republic of Congo. Our driver Mandela insisted he could get permission to take us over the border into DRC. Reluctantly we did get to walk over the border but only after many, many questions were asked to both Mandela and us.

What a difference a few yards can make!

Men with guns were everywhere making us feel very uncomfortable - we were all so relieved when we were back on Ugandan soil. We had all felt very intimidated.

I hired a car for four days and a driver Mandela who I had met in 2011, and we set off at 9.30 am to meet Denis again. Denis had taken a Boda Boda (motorbike) all the way from Ishaka to meet us at a certain roadside venue, so that he could guide us to his home which was about ½ hours' drive away. We were 1 hour late in meeting him, but he was still waiting at the roadside and by now it was 1.45pm.

After 3 years of not seeing each other it was an emotional meeting which took place at the roadside with big hugs between us. With his guidance we travelled on to reach his home where we were greeted by his parents and many other members of his family. A small meal had been prepared for us and after eating, Denis took me to another small building a few yards from the dining room and showed me where he slept with other brothers and this too was where he did his studying. It was a small very dark room lit only by an oil lamp.

We later drove to Buhoma where Mandela and I were to stay in the Green Tree B&B for the 2 nights. Our evening meal was simply chips!! Denis and Jeremiah, who had previously joined us, then left for home in pouring rain on a Boda Boda. I lent Denis my raincoat as he did not possess one. Later he claimed it as his own and wore it for several years.

The following morning at 7am a bucket of hot water for me to use for washing my self was delivered to my door. After breakfast Denis arrived on a Boda Boda. Later we drove back to his home and I was taken on a tour of the very small Nyakeina school just a few yards from the house. As guests of honour we were entertained by all the children who sang songs in English and danced in front of us. We were also invited to join in the dancing when, suddenly there was a huge thunderstorm and we all dashed for shelter.

A huge lunch had been prepared at Denis's home for the whole family and because I was sponsoring him, I was a VIP guest therefore a chicken and one of Denis's goats had been killed and cooked for the special occasion.

After lunch I gave out gifts for the small children and other members of the family. Shirts and ties for the men and although they had been previously worn, they were all delighted to own one. For the ladies, costume jewellery, beautiful perfumed soap and silk scarves. The children also were delighted with some toys. For the remainder of the afternoon Denis took Mandela and me around the small piece of land which his Father owns. We viewed the small tea plantation and coffee bushes, also there were Yams growing and banana trees both Matoke and Yellow.

We saw the spring where daily the water had to be collected from. This was at the bottom of a very steep hill. Often while we were out and about, we saw children as young as three years old carrying large yellow jerry cans of water on their heads. Mandela and I later drove back to our B&B for the night.

The next morning, we were up bright and early at 6am and after breakfast we drove to Nyakeina village where we were to pick up Denis. To my surprise there was not only Denis waiting for us but Labour, Chrispus and Pius a half-brother, all piled into the back of our 5-seater car. I learned that they were on their way back to school in Butogoto. It seemed that they had been allowed home for the VIP celebration!

After dropping them off at school we carried on our journey reaching Ishaka at 12 noon where we checked into the Headland Hotel. Denis had booked each of our accommodation in advance, which was really helpful. He then took me to see his new accommodation a 2 roomed flat near the university, where he provided us with lunch. It was there where I met his very best friend Ojok, who was in his final year of studying medicine.

That evening I took all of us to the 5* Crane Hotel for Dinner, paid for by my friend Gordon who had given me another £50 to treat us to a meal. His gift also provided us with a second meal the following evening at the same hotel. The two budding doctors, both from impoverished families had never set foot inside such a place and were so appreciative of this generous and wonderful experience. To me the hotel was probably like a 3* in England, but to the others it was sheer luxury.

The following day Ojok invited us to take breakfast in his rooms. The rest of that day the two boys spent taking me on a grand tour of the Kampala International University and the Teaching Hospital. They were both shocked and surprised when I told them I was appalled at some of the conditions in the hospital!! Of course, they had never seen any other so couldn't compare standards.

The next morning Mandela and I departed Ishaka to be waved off after a huge hug by both boys.

Our 3½ hour journey back to Kisoro took us through banana and tea plantations and beautiful mountainous scenery in glorious sunshine.

Back at Countryside Hotel I was greeted just like a long-awaited friend by 2 of the girl staff. My heavy suitcase was hoisted onto the top of the head of one of them and carried with ease into my room.

The next three days were spent visiting several ACE supported schools, plus a visit for me to Vision SS to see the four students being sponsored by my friends in Scarborough who had sent special gifts for them.

On 1st October at 9am Angela, Vic and myself said goodbye to our friends in Kisoro and set off on our drive to the Queen Elizabeth National Park. We arrived at 2.15pm. where we had been given free accommodation for two nights in a Rangers Lodge. Angela had been given this by a Ugandan friend called Charles Etoru as a thank you for all the work done there and for the money she has raised for the Ugandan ACE schools and children.

After unpacking we had afternoon tea in our lodge, then walked to the area which overlooks the Kasinga Channel. On the far bank we could see a family of elephants and hippos enjoying themselves in and around the water. Later that evening back in our lodge we all got so excited as two elephants walked just yards from us through our garden, SUCH EXCITEMENT!!

The next morning having enjoyed our breakfast we made our way to a very poor school on the border of the park. This is being supported by Charles and his colleagues.

At 4pm that afternoon, we were again very privileged to be taken on a 3 ¼ hours Safari Ride with a tour guide. We had a wonderful time and were very lucky to see all the animals who live in the QENP - except Lions. They were so well hidden when we were on our drive.

Following dinner in the Tempo restaurant that evening, we drove back to our lodge, and on arrival we were greeted by a huge Hippo' in our front garden. Another exciting experience.

Our last morning, we were up at 6am, ate breakfast and packed what remained of our luggage into the car which was very much lighter now having given out all the equipment for the nine ACE schools, plus our personal gifts to friends.

We left QENP for the 7 ½ hour long journey back to Entebbe where we stayed overnight. The next morning, we were all up very early as Angela and Vic were catching an early flight. I wanted to say my goodbye to them as I would not see them again for at least a year. Penzance, in Cornwall, where they live, being hundreds of miles away from Scarborough, North Yorkshire.

My flight did not leave until late that evening. So, I spent the day at the Entebbe Zoo where I was delighted to see another Shoebill very close in an enclosure. Feeling hungry I ordered a plate of chips for my lunch and although there was only one other couple at the lakeside café, it took over an hour before I had my chips served. I have learned that "Nothing is done in a hurry in Uganda"!

David picked me up later that day and took me into a beautiful garden overlooking Lake Victoria to have cool drinks whilst waiting to travel to the airport for my flight home. It would be nearly four years later before I would visit Uganda and see Denis again.

CHAPTER 8

Fund Raising

I had been involved in fund raising over many years for various charities, however I was just one member of a committee of many people. After Angela and the people in Uganda had gone to great lengths checking that Denis was genuine and securing him a place in a senior school, I wanted to raise a little money for the charity ACE as a thank you to Angela.

My first solo event on 11th June 2010 was a Coffee Morning which I held in my home and it was attended by neighbours and friends and my two daughters helped in the kitchen. To my amazement I made a wonderful £240 which I sent to ACE. Encouraged by my success I decided to do a Soup and Sandwich lunch on 20th Nov 2010 to raise yet more for ACE. My daughter Katharine having much more floor space in her home than me, agreed to me holding the event there. The two of us each made a different flavoured soup and prepared an assortment of sandwiches and homemade cakes. On this successful occasion we raised a very pleasing £214 and again sent it to ACE.

By this time my Bangladeshi friend called Nahar had become very keen to help and she offered to prepare and serve an Indian lunch in her home. I quickly sold all the tickets for all these events and for the Indian Lunch. We had even more people wanting to support such events. We raised £322 this time.!!

In August 2011 I decided to be more adventurous and organise a Strawberry and Cream tea in my garden. My two daughters and son-in-law's and the grand children who were available helped me erect the gazebos and we put out lots of tables and chairs. Each person was served with a small dish of strawberries and cream with a delicious homemade buttered scone on the side and a lovely cup of Yorkshire tea! We also ran a raffle. This was a very happy day for everyone who came resulting in raising a magnificent £565 for ACE.

By March 2012 I sold my house and downsized to a bungalow which had a much smaller garden and was in a completely different area of the town to where I had lived for 46 years.

After I had settled into my new home, I decided that one way to get to know my neighbours and those people who lived in my cul-de-sac was to have an 'Open House' coffee morning. I would make no charge but suggested if they wished they could make a donation to ACE.

Expecting just a few to attend I was pleasantly surprised to see lots of new neighbours and some of my friends. At the end of the day there was £165 in the charity box. I delighted in sending another donation to ACE.

Since the move into my bungalow and having a much smaller garden we have held the Annual Strawberry and Cream Teas in my daughter Katharine's very large and attractive garden, which luckily is just across the road from my home, so my grandsons and son-in-law can lift all the spare tables and many chairs etc from my garage where they are stored and carry them across the road and lift them over the hedge into her garden and also return them after the event.

Also, after the move the two annual lunches have been held in my home. For the first one I thought I could seat approximately 16 people, but 18 arrived, I soon found places for them to sit at and there was also ample food for them. Gradually more and more people wanted to come to my lunches and with careful planning I found that now I can seat a maximum of 34, yes 34 people, using every available space. On the actual day of a lunch I have my two willing daughters and a couple of friends to help in the kitchen, serve the food, and wash all the dirty dishes and sell the raffle tickets for me.

Over the years we have served a good variety of dishes.: - Bangers, Mash and Peas; Roast Salmon, new potatoes and green veg; Chili Con Carne and rice; Beef casserole; Fish pie and Chicken casserole to name but a few!! We have served a wonderful variety of desserts, at first always made by me, however as the support has increased my neighbours and friends have also produced some delicious ones. Pavlova, Eton mess, Trifle, Apple crumble also Apple pies, etc, etc.

After many years of raising funds first for ACE alone I found that Denis who had started his studying at University, needed more financial support, so half the takings of each event have been sent to ACE and the other half has gone towards the fees and living expenses for Denis.

CHAPTER 9

Presentations and Talks

Around this time, I began to be asked if I would go to talk to different groups of people about my experiences in Uganda and how I had met and become involved with supporting a young man there. I have spoken to Ladies Evening groups, Rotary clubs, at WI (Women's Institute) and the University of the Third Age, usually being given a small donation from each. By 2019 I had raised a grand total of £5,662 for the ACE charity.

During the years since meeting Denis and hearing about his success at school and his progress at KIU, many of my friends and acquaintances, have given me donations for him, ranging from £10, £50, £100 and even £500. Even strangers have given money.

CHAPTER 10

University

During his first year at University Denis discovered that he was having to pay out lots of his money on purchasing copies of each of the lectures. He now needed a Laptop to download all this information. We soon realised that a Uni student cannot manage without one. So, the money was sent out to Denis to buy one, as neither letter nor parcel can be posted out to Uganda from the UK, they disappear without trace. Corruption is rife there!!

At this time, I was also given several second -hand medical books for Denis by my own GP also from a newly retired doctor friend. Fortunately, I managed to get these taken out by a lady called Gill who also runs a charity in the south western corner of Uganda. She met Denis at his University gate and handed them over to him. On another occasion Gill carried out a Tablet for him and several more books. These kind gestures were very much appreciated by Denis and me.

After visiting Uganda in 2014 Denis continued with his studies with lectures in the University and practical experience in the University hospital. At the end of each Semester they would not be able to go home for a holiday as they were sent off to hospitals in different areas of the country to gain further practical experience, because the university teaching hospital was small and therefore did not have a lot of patients.

Denis spent time in locations both near and far away from Ishaka. Some of these were, Mubende, Fort Portal, Hoima, Itojo, Mitoma and Kitagata. During his 4th year while at Kitagata in September 2015, he was able to watch a doctor perform several Caesarean operations. In theatre one day they had 3 caesareans to perform, the surgeon performed two and then asked Denis to do the third, and with a little assistance he delivered a beautiful baby girl weighing 2.9kg. Denis was thrilled!!

After my return home Denis and I kept in touch almost every weekend by sending an email to each other. He would tell me how his semester was progressing, at times how members of his large family were and about the growing of crops.

At one time I was told about people in the Ishaka area catching swarms of Crickets/Grasshoppers and frying them before eating them, which I found amazing. Apparently, they are full of protein and treated as a delicacy.

At the end of each semester Denis would sit the examinations and without exception when the results came out, he would be placed in the top three of his year. During the 5 ½ years at University he never had to re sit an exam, his commitment to studying was so great.

When writing to Denis, if I had been to anywhere of interest in the UK or on holiday to another country, I would tell him details about where I was. A few of the places I visited during these years were a tour of Scotland, Hawaii, Rome, Athens, Pathos and several of the Canary Islands. He was keen to hear about different parts of the world and how they live, and I always sent an abundance of photographs.

I also told him about my family, my two daughters, Katharine and Jane, two son-in-laws and my five lovely grandchildren, about their schools and their out of school activities. Over time our emails, at first brief, became longer and longer.

During the summer of 2015 I received a message from one of the trustees of ACE called Janet, who at that time coordinated the sending and receiving of all letters from the ACE students to their sponsor and the return letters from sponsor to student. Janet had earlier that year set up, THE VISION. The Newsletter of the ACE Sponsorship Scheme. Janet requested me to ask Denis if he would be prepared to write about his early life and the effect qualifying as a doctor would have on himself and his community. This was to take th e form of an Interview for this Newsletter. Denis felt it was an honour to be asked and on the next page is what he wrote for the "Interview with Denis Musasizi."

Dear my lovely Janet.

How are you doing there in the UK and how is everyone Feeling.

First of all, I take this opportunity to thank you, and all the ACE trustees for the trust and love you have for me to consider me as the next participant in the ACE Newsletter, the Organisation that has actually brought most of us from very far to where we are now and rest assured of a brilliant future. Again I have to make this apology to you for having not really replied in time as I expected but you also understand school life and especially this life of being a medical student. You can't know what time you will get a patient with what condition, meaning you have to attend to a patient at any hour he/she comes and go and read about the condition you have managed with your doctor/lecturer/consultant. So I have to tell you that I was in the Kitagata hospital where I was posted for my holiday hospital practice and I was supposed to come back to campus on Sunday but because of some unavoidable circumstances , have just arrived today morning and I have to start doing everything to prepare myself for my 4th year 1st semester. Which has bean today.

Now to answer ACE Interview Questions,

1. Tell me a bit about your life before you met your sponsor and began at Vision school; what education did you have? Where did that take place? And what is your home like?

My life before I met my sponsor was generally not good as I started my primary education in 1998 at the age of 8 years. We could generally start our education at an older age because of several reasons

A, long distance from home to the nearest school which is about 7km from home and the school is called Kanyashande primary school where I studied P1 to P7.

B,Acting as maids. In Africa, usually you are the one to look after the brother or sister who follows.So like me,I am followed by a sister called Moreen (unfortunately got married in her s2) and I had to make sure she doesn't cry at any one time while my mother is in gardens digging. Every brother of mine would do it for the next sibling.

C, Food and school fees. All Pupils from p1 to p7 used to leave home from 7:00 am and reach school by 8:00am, however, p1 and p2 used to come back home at 1:00 pm and we could reach this time before we eat anything meaning someone to begin school had to be old to withstand this hunger. Then P3 to P7 coming back home would be 4:00pm meaning we had to pack food in buckets like matooke,sweet potatoes etc. Then also at times when a parent would be having more than 5 children in primary,then the others had to be home waiting for the others to finish meanwhile cultivating to create more food for them and some would stop in secondary school or primary. A case in point, Obed our 1st born stopped in secondary and moses 2nd born in p6 then Ephraim got chance completed grade 3 in primary teaching and Onesmus 4th born stopped at p7 but after like 5 years out of school, as God helps just like me,he got someone to sponsor him and is now having diploma in tourism and hotel management but later got a job in UWA, as a tour guide in Mgahinga and Bwindi Impenetrable NP. Isaiah the 5th born stopped at p7 .Jeremiah the 6th born was lucky and my Dad pushed him also for teaching, grade 3 primary education just as Ephraim, then me the 7th born,I was lucky too that I was passing highly as I never repeated in any class apart from p1 which I attended 1998 and 1999.This was because in 1998 3rd term my Dad made me sit for one term chasing birds from eating beans,then started afresh p1 again in 1999,Nevertheless, in Nov 2005 completed p7 with 14 aggregates.My brother Ephraim was a teacher already and paid for me fees from s1 to s4 in Butogota trinity college as my Dad was looking after the siblings and Jeremiah in primary teachers college.

So though trinity college by then wasn't a good school, I tried hard and passed well my O'level as I was the 1st in the whole s4 class 2009 UNEB and got 32 aggregates a 1st grade and the second person to me had 45 agg 2nd grade and many more made 3rd grades,4th ,5th and others failed with 7th and 9th grades.Now it so happened that I went to Bwindi NP in my S 4 vacation to act as a porter so as I can get some money for books, where I met my Sponsor Mrs VALERIE HUMPHREYS where we conversed together ,told her everything about my life and left me with her email address. Now because I had passed well and from such a poor O'level school,my parents and brothers were so concerned and decided that I should go to a somehow good school for A'level.In Uganda, Advanced level is taken to be for bright people and those from rich families who afterwards go for University Whereas those who are academically ill or are from poor families go to institutions for 1 or 2 years and have a job to do.

So they decided I go to Bishop Comboni college Kambuga for A'level in 2010 where I studied for one term and we failed to raise the money any more,or if they continued with me,it would mean all other brothers and sister stopping and would again fail raising lots of money I pay at University.So I was going to stop in s5 1st term or look for a cheap A'Level school which you can't get as all A'level schools are expensive. Here is where the blessings of God came to me and a lady of God Mrs VALERIE HUMPHREYS offered to sponsor me from s5 2nd term in Kisoro vision school up to s6 which I completed in 2011 Nov and was able to get all the principle passes at A'level and qualified to go to university at any course corresponding with my combination at A'level. I decided to go to Kampala international university western campus where I got admission and she allowed me to go and still sponsor me from 2012 Sept up to now and I have much hopes that with God's mercy,I will even complete my course,as long as I am with her!!!!!!!! . Now all the brothers gather money from their pockets to pay for Labour the 9th born now at saint marys' Kabale s5 doing PCB/Sub maths.and Crspus the 10th and last born in Trinity,the same school I attended for A'level and he is now in s2.They are all doing well.The 8th born is Moreen who stopped in s2 and got married.So we are 10 children,9 boys and 1 girl all from one father and one mother.

My home isn't a good one, my dad having a temporary house made from reeds, poles and mad soil and then roofed iron sheets but I hope everything will be fine when I complete my education.My dad has a few goats,tea plantation about 1 acre, about 20 plants of coffee and about ½ acre of banana plantation and this is where he raises the money to support the entire family.

2. What are you doing now?

I am now preparing to start off my 4th year 1st semester at Campus. And I am a medical student doing bachelors of medicine and bachelors of surgery.I do go to class to attend lectures and have also time to go to the wards in the hospital to practice as the exams we do here are both theory/written, VIV/oral and clinical/practical work. However,during holidays,we are posted to other many hospital about 3 students in each group so as we can get more experience,exposure and see many cases.forexample I have been in Kitagata hospital in Bushenyi for my holiday practice and has just arrive today.

Of course after lectures, and ward practice,I go and prepare my own food in my own house which I rent in Ishaka Bushenyi district but just near campus.

3. What are your plans for the future?

Well, thank you very much for this good question.

My future plans are obviously becoming a doctor and benefit myself, my/ our family and my community at large.

4. What effect will becoming a doctor have on a: your family. b. your community and c. yourself.

Well, starting with myself,

Becoming a doctor will enable me have good health as we know he who has health has wealth, it will enable me afford all the basic needs that I will want because obviously I will be having the money and then it will make me popular and famous because I will be having the money to move to many places as required and necessary and again the people I will be treating or working with have to know me.

Then with My family, Of course they will also have good health because they are the first people I will help while emphasizing health in the community, I have to try eradicate poverty in the family through uplifting my brothers, nieces and nephews. This I will achieve through helping everyone in the family get educated, producing a few children so as everyone can get the right to education and provide them exposure.

And then to the community, I have to act examporary by showing how to maintain or promote health in the community and treat communicable diseases, advise them to prevent lifestyle diseases and most importantly like DM, Hypertension and HIV/AIDS Infection which is a real threat to Uganda and this can hinder developments in the community. Of course like in people with already HIV/AIDS I have to advise on the taking of drugs to reduce on viral load and be faithful to partners or have always a protected sex.

Again I have to make sure I advise the community to engage in income generating projects so as they can raise money to make them afford health services, education services to their children, thus eradicating poverty. If possible I can again try to create employments to people for example if I put up a clinic, I can employ more than 10 people who would otherwise be home jobless both health workers and non-health workers like accountants, human resource managers, cleaners etc. Both can earn something thus enhancing developments, that's just one example but I will be ready to do as many projects as possible to benefit every party in the community.

I can't stop here but have to go ahead and visit small to large health centers and advise on the things we should have in different facilities and departments. Then visit schools as well and see the health standards there as this is a sensitive area, where we have people who are becoming future presidents,professors,doctors,teachers etc and I have to observe it both in health and social aspects. Like having good water sources, good accommodations, washing their clothings, hand washing before eating, and when it comes to ladies, I have to encourage on how to maintain their health while in menstrual periods and etc....

I am sorry I have answered you a lot, but it's just because you asked me obvious things and above all my area of interest.

I think I am a good leader who can even in future stand in parliament to fight for the health of Ugandans' have to tell you that since 2012 when I started 1.1 at campus, I have been a class president leading my fellow students well, where some of my colleagues developed a feeling that we should begin an organization to sensitize about health in villages about once or twice in a holiday in different villages. So they had asked me to lead the student organization but of course we couldn't progress because of limited funds. So anyway, this never affected me because my education comes first but this showed me that while leading the class, I was doing the right thing. I am now a class advisor at 23 years now going to make 24 in 10th October.

So I have a lot and a lot to do for myself, family and community at large, but just to mention a few for the interest of time.

I know it's now a book and will burden you read it but I am very sorry, it's just because of the much love I have for ACE, and recalling where it brought me from.

Otherwise God bless you, ACE ,founder(S) trustees, the sponsors, the ACE sponsored children and all its well-wishers for the job they have done and are continuing to do.

With God being our Protector all of us shall succeed; AMEN

Kind regards Denis Musasizi Valerie Humphreys' African Grandson Dr.to be soon.

Sponsored by Mrs. VALERIE HUMPHREYS

CHAPTER 11

Meeting Doctor Chander Shukla (Dr Tony)

During the summer of 2017 I took my youngest grandson on a nursery school outing to a play farm along with a group of other parents and grandparents. While the children were playing in a large sandpit, I sat next to a father of two children who was also in our group.

We began to talk, and he told me he was a doctor and worked in Scarborough hospital. This prompted me to tell him about how I was supporting a young man in Uganda who was studying to become a doctor. I mentioned I was hoping to be able to get Denis to the UK to do his Internship after he had completed his time at University. I was surprised but very pleased when Dr Tony said he would like to try to help as he has already assisted a couple of Indian doctors to come to England. We kept in touch.

It was around this time that Denis and I started to talk about what he would need to be able to come to the UK for further study or for a brief holiday. We realized he would need a Passport. Denis told me he had been advised it would be much easier to be given one while he was still studying at University rather than after. Once again that needed more money which I sent to him. He applied, again having to travel to Kampala to put in his application and later to go back once more to collect his Passport in person. All extremely long and expensive journeys when one lives or studies in the south western part of Uganda!!

Denis was due to complete his course and qualify as a Doctor in February 2018 so Dr Tony and I got together to see how we were going to be able to help him acquire a VISA so he could do his Internship in the UK . We tried many avenues over the next few weeks.

I asked for advice from my local MP as he had at one time been our Foreign Office Minister. Initially, he seemed really keen to help, but shortly after declined any help, saying that someone from Uganda would not go back there after his visa had expired. I assured him that I would be paying for Denis's return airfare and that he only wanted to acquire more advanced medical knowledge here, as he desperately wants to save lives and help his own very poor people in the poverty stricken areas where his home is in the south western corner of Uganda.

Dr Tony went to a lot of trouble enquiring at the local hospital about a possible Internship course there. He even offered free accommodation in his own home for the duration of Denis's stay.

I wrote a personal letter explaining that I had been sponsoring Denis since 2010 and would be accountable for all his living expenses while in this country.

Denis completed the appropriate VISA forms and travelled to Kampala to personally hand them in to be processed.

After all our efforts he was told that he would never be given a visa to come here for Internship. However, he could apply for a six months holiday VISA.

So again, Dr Tony and I wrote letters of invitation and Denis filled in all the appropriate forms and once more travelled to Kampala to the application office to hand them in and pay a fee for the second time. He was told it would take approx. 3 weeks before he would receive a reply.

One Friday morning Denis received a reply saying he could pick it up on the Monday at the office. Once again, he travelled all the way to Kampala, went to the office and nervously and very anxious awaited to be served. After waiting some 'hours' with very high hopes, the letter was given to him. On opening the envelope, he was devastated – the application had once again been rejected

On seeing his great disappointment a lady in the office comforted him and then suggested that it might help if he could get help financially first to set up a small clinic in his name to run after he had taken his Internship in Uganda. Then to try again to get a VISA to come to the UK for further training. She said the authorities would then realise that he would go back home to run his clinic.

At this point in time both Dr Tony and I thought this would be the best idea rather than wasting any more money. Altogether the costs had run into well over £300 with nothing to show for it.

CHAPTER 12

Further Medical Knowledge

Denis went home for Christmas in 2017 and celebrated the new year 2018 with his family. Shortly after, he returned to his university to revise in preparation for his final exams. These began on 5th February and ended on 16th February. Denis sat a total of 11 exams on medicine and 11 on surgery. He then had to wait approximately 2 weeks for the results to be out.

At the end of February 2018, he was handed the transcripts of his five and half year's attendance at Kampala International University. From semester one in 2012 to his final one on 16th February 2018. On that memorable date he became a fully qualified Doctor. However, his graduation ceremony would not take place until June 23rd, 2018 in Kampala. Also, his Internship would not begin until the October 2018 if taken in Uganda. This looked very likely now he had been refused a visa.

Denis could have gone home after he had qualified and wasted his time doing menial work in the area. However, he wanted to further his medical knowledge and had been given the chance to work in a private hospital called Ntungamo, a doctor's referral hospital where he had been helped by the Dean of Kampala International University to contact the Director. The director said he would accept

Denis to go for further training. However, the doctor would charge 500,000 ugs per month for Denis to accompany him on his duties. He would be assigned to a senior doctor who he could always shadow, and he would give Denis hands on in all procedures and operations.

To be able to take up this offer it meant he would again need financial support. He was to be given a room in which to sleep for free but his daily requirements like food etc had to be paid for. Once again, my fund raising continued!! After spending very valuable 'hands on' time at Ntungamo hospital Denis went on doing volunteering work in other government clinics.

Most times as soon as he arrived at a government clinic 1V to volunteer the government paid doctor at the said clinic found Dr Denis to be very conscientious and capable, would then go to his own private clinic to make more money for himself. Denis continued to work in such clinics helping to deliver babies naturally and carried out so many caesarean section deliveries that after a while he lost count. He continued doing this work until my arrival in Entebbe on June 20th, 2018.

CHAPTER 13

Graduation 23rd June 2018

During the spring of 2018 the date was set for Denis's Graduation Ceremony, and as I had promised so many years before that if he got to a university and then graduated, I would be there to witness him graduating.

Together we began to make plans for my visit. On my previous visits to Uganda with ACE all the plans for travel and accommodation had been organised by Angela with help from David the Ugandan man who works for ACE part time. As I was going on my own for this visit, I thought I would have to ask for David's help and assistance again. However, when I mentioned this to Denis, he requested me to please trust him, saying that he was very capable of arranging all our plans, so we worked together. I was extremely impressed as Denis saved me many thousands of Ugandan shillings less than David had quoted us!!

Denis had been recommended a man whose name was Boss who owned a car hire business in Ishaka. He checked out Boss's credentials which were excellent, before arranging all the costings with him, and together we came to an agreement. I needed to hire both car and driver for my entire stay in Uganda. Denis and myself also needed accommodation booking in each of the towns where we would be staying for a few days of my visit.

In Kisoro I requested Denis to book us rooms at Countryside guest house where I had stayed on my two previous visits. While visiting his parents' home near Bwindi Denis would sleep at home and he booked me into the Bwindi Forest Safari Resort Cottages, in Butogota, just a few miles away.

In Kampala we needed to stay for four nights and at first it was becoming rather a problem as not only had we to find rooms for Denis and myself but also for his Father and Mother who were to come to Kampala for the Graduation Ceremony. This was going to be a huge adventure for his parents as they had never in their lives before travelled further than a few miles from their own district and they lived in a small house built of mud and sticks. Denis had suggested one or two guest houses to me but on looking at pictures of them on Google I knew that they would not be suitable for me to stay in.

I decided to find accommodation in Kampala myself by looking on the internet. One day rather than looking for guest houses I decided to look at apartments and houses to rent for vacations. It did not take me long before I came across a house which called itself a Luxurious Holiday Home.

Many pictures of it were displayed on the site. It had three double bedrooms and two bathrooms and would be ideal for all of us to stay together. Best of all the price per night was extremely reasonable. I sent Denis details of what I proposed together with pictures and he agreed it sounded a great idea.

So, I booked and paid for the home for the four of us, on the internet. I was very pleasantly surprised the very next day when I received a mobile telephone call from the owner of the home, who told me he was speaking from Canada where he lived. His name was Ru. He wanted to introduce himself and tell me about the Luxurious Home and what we could expect there. I told him I lived in England and that I would be travelling to Uganda to attend the Graduation of my sponsored student, Denis Musasizi, who had recently qualified as a Doctor.

I advised him that Denis and his parents would be travelling from Bwindi on the day of my arrival and that they would arrive around 5/6pm at the house. Then later during the evening Denis and the driver of the car would travel to Entebbe airport to collect me on my arrival at 10 .20pm.

Ru said he would e-mail me all the instructions and directions to get to the house after Denis and family reached the outskirts of Kampala. He also gave me two telephone numbers of his two-lady staff who he said lived on the premises. He asked if I would tell Denis to phone the ladies on the day prior to their travel. I was also told that he employed a night watchman from 6pm until 6am each night who would patrol the premises with an Alsatian dog. I forwarded all these instructions to Denis. All our plans for my visit were now in place.

I travelled alone to Uganda, as promised many years ago to attend the Graduation of my, at first, sponsored teenager, now a young man, a qualified medical doctor. My suitcase and hand luggage were packed to capacity not only with my clothes and personal belongings but also with gifts from local Sponsors for their child at Vision school in Kisoro.

On hearing that I personally knew a young mother in Kisoro who had very little money and was expecting a second baby, a young mother in Scarborough gave me lots of clothes and nappies and toiletries for her, as she said she had been given far too many for her own new-born baby. I became emotionally moved by this very generous gesture.

Other items I was carrying were small toys for three children I had met previously on my visits to see Denis's family. Also packed, were many toilet soaps, toothpaste, pens, pencils, and rulers and items of costume jewellery. Lastly, I had items of food to be used while we were going to be staying in the luxury home in Kampala.

Cheese and biscuits, corned beef, hot chocolate, homemade marmalade, an assortment of biscuits and sweets. As I write these details, I wonder how I packed them all in!!

I departed home at 1.15 am on the 19th June 2018 driven by my daughter Jane in her car to Manchester airport. She dropped me at departures and after hugs and a big thank you to her for driving me, she immediately set off on her journey back to Scarborough. Feeling sleepy on the journey home she had to stop for a short while for a nap in a lay-by before carrying on with her journey home.

My short flight to Brussels, a wait, then a further flight to Entebbe went to plan and I finally arrived on time at 10.20 pm. I had the usual wait to go through passport and visa control, then to collect my luggage, put it onto a trolley and push it through to arrivals exit. As I walked out of the arrivals area I looked around and there was Denis standing in the near distance looking across at me. No longer was I being met by an uneducated teenager, but by a very self-assured, mature young man. My heart missed a beat as we walked towards each other for our long-awaited meeting. It being four years since we had last met.

I was introduced to Boss the driver of our car; my luggage was put in and we were on our journey to the luxurious home where we were to stay for the first four nights.

As we travelled, they told me of the trauma they had experienced once they reached the outskirts of Kampala to find the home. As instructed by the owner Ru, Denis had tried to telephone the two-lady staff, only to be told they had nothing to do with the house. The directions we had been given said they were to turn right/left at a certain named petrol filling station, however there was no such named filling station in the area. The named one had long gone.!! After one hour of searching to find the home they decided to stop and ask a boda boda driver for directions. They paid him to guide them to the home. They would never have found it by themselves because it was off the beaten track and on an unmade very rocky bumpy road.

At last they were outside the premises which they knew were right as they had a picture of the house and its large gates. They rang the bell, banged on the gates, tried to telephone again but to no avail. After a long hour at last the night watchman arrived and let them into the grounds and house.

It transpired that the lady staff I had been given telephone numbers for had both left, and two new staff were there with of course different telephone numbers to the ones we had been given. We were not expected!!

The furniture was under wraps. However, they were all made welcome. Boss had set off from his home in Ishaka, extremely early in the day, picked up Denis and then his parents from near their home in Bwindi, also a cousin and her 2 yrs. old daughter. Unbeknown to me they were all going to sleep in the house.

Denis with Boss to drive him, were now running very late to get to the airport in time to meet me. They had quickly dropped off the rest of the family in the house and all the luggage before setting off for the airport. They had only just reached there in time to meet me.
My luggage was quickly put into the car and we were off!

By the time we arrived at The Luxurious Home it was well past midnight and even though his parents were in bed Denis insisted he must tell them of my arrival, and they got up to come and greet me. He made a drink for us and shortly after we all went to bed. It did not take much persuasion to get Boss our driver to sleep the night on one of the large sofas rather than to go off to find accommodation in the area.

This house did indeed turn out to be quite grand. It had originally been a colonial home of some standing and stood in its own grounds with high walls surrounding it with barbed wire on the top and huge double solid gates at its entrance. There was even a gateman's room at the side of these gates. There were servants living quarters around the back of the main house, and well-maintained gardens on three sides of the main building for us to enjoy. The huge lounge was very well furnished and had an open plan dining room. The kitchen was well stocked with all the equipment we needed, and the two lady staff couldn't do enough for us during our four days stay.

My bedroom was huge and in it the most enormous bed I have ever seen, beautiful mahogany wardrobes and cupboards and sets of drawers. There was a dressing room, and this led into an on-suite bathroom with bath as well as a shower, hand basin, toilet and bidet. There were two other double bedrooms a shower room with hand basin and a separate toilet All the Ugandan family had been amazed when they arrived and entered this beautiful accommodation. Especially Denis's parents who had never travelled in their whole lives before.

One day while we were all sitting at the table having a meal, Denis's father jokingly said he expected his son, now a doctor to "One day buy his parents a home like this!!" I was delighted to have found this unusual accommodation for us all to stay in together, and had the feeling that as a family, male and female, different nationalities, languages and traditions, it had brought us all together.

During one meal while all seated together the parents were fascinated to watch me pushing some vegetable onto my fork with my knife. Of course, they had never seen anyone use a fork and knife before.!!

On the 21st June, we all relaxed after our long journeys of the previous day. During the afternoon Boss drove Denis and myself into the city to go to the bank to exchange my English money into Ugandan shillings. On this short journey I began to realise what a terrible city Kampala is to drive in, with traffic jams everywhere and hundreds, yes hundreds of boda boda's travelling in every direction amongst the cars. Some with four or even five people on one machine.

That day was my birthday and unbeknown to me Julianah, Denis's cousin had made and brought with her a two-tiered iced birthday cake which had been carried in a large cardboard box. During our evening meal this was ceremoniously unpacked and put on the table and with me holding a knife they all put their hands on the top of mine as we cut the cake. Then Happy Birthday was sung to me in English. This was such a wonderful surprise.

The next day we went to pay for and collect Denis's Graduation Cap and Gown from the university. We also went shopping to buy a white shirt, a pair of Clarks shoes and a leather belt for him to wear on such an occasion. That evening Julianah and Denis cooked a traditional Ugandan evening meal for us all, and after the two-lady staff did all the washing up.

CHAPTER 14

June 23rd 2018 - Graduation Day

Valerie, left and Denis, right on his graduation day, June 23rd 2018 in Kampala.

Graduation day had at last arrived for Denis who had worked so tirelessly since enrolling at Kampala International University in September 2012!

We were all up very early that morning. Unfortunately, only Denis, his Father and I would be able to attend the actual event as each graduate had only been allocated two tickets for their guests. I was so proud of Denis when I saw him dressed in his graduation outfit and took photo's before we set off for the venue.

Boss drove us to the event and as usual when travelling by car in Kampala we were held up in several traffic jams on the way. We were directed to a parking area which was a disused football pitch and field. Boss stayed with the car and we three had to climb up concrete steps which had been the seating area for the football spectators. When we arrived at the top, we were ushered towards a photo booth where photographs were taken of each of us with Denis and then the three of us together.

We then joined a very long queue going towards the official entrance of the event. Eventually we were separated by the officials, males in one line and females in another. I took out my camera and took one or two pictures of Denis and his Father standing in line. Suddenly a demand was made that we all had to hand in our cameras. I at first declined but it was made clear that no one could take their camera inside to the event. I had to give mine over to a young man. Luckily Denis told me to go and ask his name, which later turned out to be good advice.

I was standing in this very long line of ladies in extremely hot sunshine, the only white person there, when an official suddenly shouted out to me "Hey You!! come over here!". I wondered what I had done wrong. ! However he had seen my silver hair and that I was an elderly lady and did not want me to have to stand in the queue too long, so myself and also an elderly black lady were taken to the front of the line and through security and into the vast arena.

We realized that security was very thorough as the guest of honour was the President of the republic of Uganda, Mr Yoweri Kaguta Museveni.

I waited just inside for Denis's Father to join me and then we were shown to the designated area where we were to sit throughout the Graduation ceremony.

Unfortunately, we could see NOTHING of the ceremonial platform at all as we were positioned along with other parents and guests at the far side of the site and around a corner!

Gradually the grounds filled up until over 6000 people were inside. I never set eyes on another white person that day but must also say that at no time did I feel uncomfortable or conspicuous. In anticipation we waited for the ceremony to start but nothing happened. We waited and waited for what must have been about 1 ½ hours and then suddenly to great grandeur music was played as the President and his entourage walked in. I could only just see the top of his hat. I was told that he never arrives at any function he attends on time.
Such bad manners, I thought to myself!

Denis later told me what happened during the main part of the ceremony. The graduates all sat around for what seemed like hours, then one by one their names were called out by The Dean of Clinical Medicine and Dentistry, Professor Robinson Ssebuwufu. He told me that no scrolls were handed to the graduates, neither were they given a hand shake as would have been customary in Britain or the USA. We only realised the ceremony had ended when people started to get up and leave. We sat there for a while, I thought that Denis would be looking for us. However, Denis's Dad then stood up to leave so I had to follow. We could not converse as neither could speak the others language and we went out of the grounds to wait for Denis.

While waiting for him, I went to the place where I had been told we should collect our cameras. I found utter chaos, literally hundreds of people were pushing and shoving towards two huge boxes which contained the cameras and mobile phones. A line or queue would have made it very simple! I panicked as I was pushed around among all these large young men. However, after some time a kind man asked me what I was waiting for and I told him. My camera was in a red case and had been taken by the certain named man. His name was called out and my camera appeared wrapped up in clingfilm with the price of 100,000ugs on it, which I was supposed to pay to be given it back. No way was I going to pay anything, and it was just as well that I had no money on me that day as Denis had it with him! Eventually without further ado it was given to me. What a relief!!

74

When Denis did not appear, we made our way back to the car. An incident happened here which when recalled at breakfast the next day to Denis's Mother by her husband, caused much laughter for us all.

For when we had reached the very steep concrete steps to go down to our car , there being no handrail to hold, Denis's father very gallantly put out his hand for me to hold and the two of us negotiated the steps together, the language being no barrier!!

Unbeknown to Denis's father and I, the Graduates had gone into a special room where they were to take the Hippocratic oath. They waited for well over an hour and then in alphabetical order (Musasizi Denis) "MD" for Denis, they each in turn held in their hand a Holy Bible to swear the Hippocratic Oath.

At this point Denis told me he felt very excited but also nervous, as during the long wait for his name to be called, he imagined," What if his name was forgotten or skipped." Then finally he was sworn in and the ceremony completed, he was able to rejoice and felt extremely happy. Now he was officially Doctor Musasizi Denis. Bachelor of Medicine and Bachelor of Surgery. Later that evening all of us, Mother, Father, Julianah and 2 year old Vicky, Denis, myself and Boss all went out for an evening meal together to celebrate this wonderful achievement.

Nyakeina - Mukono
Kayonza - Kanungu
Uganda

29/6/2018

My lovely grandma Mrs Valerie humphreys, it
is a great pleasure for the 10 days we have
had together, it has been so impressive to have
you attend my graduation and to celebrate your
53rd birth day together. What a lovely moments!
It's sad, however, today to see you packing
all your luggage to fly back to the UK, I wish
we could stay together for ever but it's impossible.
So I must wish you a safe Journey, though
my eyes are Just filled up with tears, I pray
that you will be coming back to uganda soon!!
Thank you so much for bringing me up from
nobody to somebody; from a useless boy to
a respectable citizen (doctor); You have been
so kind and lovely eversince we met 2010
up to now; I do not have any way to pay you
back, but you and all our welwishers,

76

all those who have helped me through prayers, finance and any other sort of thing, I just wish you all the best and pray to the almighty God to keep you safe, healthy and fill your blessings.

God bless you all;

A merciful and safe journey as you fly back to the UK.

If God wishes, One day I will be there with you all in the UK.

Best and Kind Regards,

DR. MUSASIZI DENIS

Dr Musasizi Denis

CHAPTER 15

Journey to Nyakeina

The next morning after having breakfast together we gathered our belongings and packed them into the car, then all piled in ourselves including Julianah and Vicky. I knew we were overcrowded with myself and Boss in the front seats and the other five all in the back. However, I thought that we were just taking Julianah and Vicky to the bus station for them to travel home by bus. Little did I know that the previous night a decision had been taken for them to travel all the way to their destination in our car!! During the journey we were stopped twice by the traffic police to check the driver's documents, as so often happens in Uganda. Everyone kept really quiet especially the five in the back and it was a great relief when each time we were able to drive on!

We left our residence in Kampala at 9.30am for our very long journey to Nyakeina village in the Kanungu district where the parents live, we arrived there at 8 30 pm. After seeing them home I was driven to Butogota to the Bwindi Forest Cottages guest house where I was to stay
I was very surprised as a Chicken and chips supper had been prepared for me by the staff, Denis thought of everything!!

The following morning, not too early I was picked up and driven to the family home where we were to spend the day. After a warm welcome by many of the family we relaxed and then Boss and I were taken by Denis and shown over all the land owned by various members of the immediate family and other relatives. I found it fascinating that so many of one blood family could and did live in such close proximity to each other and on such a small piece of land.

Denis is also very knowledgeable about agriculture, having passed it as one of his A level examinations at Vision school. He gave us a running commentary about all the trees, bushes, tea plants, coffee bushes, yams, Jack fruit and banana trees, both yellow and green (Matoke).
One of his brothers makes a living out of making banana alcohol and selling it to people who come to buy it and socialize in a makeshift building. I think we would call it an English village Pub!!

After the grand tour we went back into the house where a hot lunch had been prepared for many of the family and guests. In my honour a chicken and a goat had been killed and stewed to be eaten along with matoke, beans, greens and millet.

On the 26th we had a wonderful day out taking brother Jeremiah and 4 yrs. old Patricia with us for the day. Patricia is the daughter of Denis's only sister. She had been given the day off school just so that she could be with me for the day. I had last seen her as a tiny baby on my previous visit. I did a lot of reminiscing that day as I was taken back to Bwindi and the area where my sister Anita and I had stayed in 2010 while tracking and seeing the Gorillas.

What a lot had changed in the ensuing years. In 2010 we had met in a wooden hut and been instructed about what to do and not to do while in the presence of the Gorilla family, and on our return after seeing the Gorillas we were taken into a round thatched seated area and given our certificate with date on to prove we had seen them. This had been a real adventure going up into the mountain and searching for these delightful animals.

This time instead of the hut there was a beautiful modern building with modern toilets and a very neat garden around the whole area.   I must admit I was rather disappointed to see the change and was so glad that I had been able to do this in the natural and wild state.

Also, in 2010 there had been only four or five huts selling African crafts and wooden model gorillas but in 2018 there were dozens of shops selling souvenirs of every kind along both sides of the road leading up to the modern buildings.

Another of Denis's brothers then joined us and we drove on the other side of the mountain right up to the top to a fantastic complex which had been newly built, with very expensive suites to let. A double room was $180 per night and a single $200. There was also a restaurant and a wonderful viewing area across to the Impenetrable Forest.

As locals and special guests, we were served with coffee or tea and biscuits "on the house".

A very happy day had been spent by all.

CHAPTER 16

Kisoro

The following morning Boss picked me up and we departed the Bwindi Forest Cottages guest house and picked up Denis at 8 am from the roadside near his home.

We drove through the national parks to Kisoro arriving at midday. News travels fast and almost as soon as we had arrived Mandela arrived on a boda boda to greet me. He had been my driver on my previous visit for the four days when I had travelled to see Denis at his home and University. Juliet and Allan arrived shortly after. I had met each of them on my previous visits.

All Ugandans give one such a warm welcome. We sat together with drinks and food before I went to unpack. During that afternoon Denis and I visited Standard school where all the ACE sponsored students had been moved to since my last visit. There I met Monic and Prossi and handed out gifts to them from their sponsors, Doreen and Nahar who live in Scarborough.

Our last visit that day was to the Vision Secondary school, where Denis had attended for his S5 and S6 years. There we paid a polite courtesy call on Dan Munyambabazi the Director, who was so pleased to see Dr Denis who had become one of his star pupils. Photos were taken of the "Master and his Pupil" together!!

Denis paying a courtesy call on Dan the Director of VISION school 2018

Valerie with infants at a school in Kisoro.

After breakfast the next morning we picked up Juliet and directed by her we drove out to the village of Mukibugu to visit Allan at his home. I had met Allan on all my previous visits to Uganda as he was being sponsored by Nahar Mamoon, one of my close friends.

His home turned out to be off the beaten track, so we had to walk quite a way across fields to reach it. Our car driver Boss decided he has better stay with his car as we all had the feeling that if we left it, it would be missing its wheels, wing mirrors etc by the time we arrived back. The locals were very curious seeing such a smart car in their village and came around close to look at it.

I was totally shocked when we reached the home, it was the poorest I had ever been in. We were greeted by Allan and taken inside the house. He introduced us to his sisters and brothers who were standing around. There was a low wooden table in the middle of a tiny room and wooden seats around it for us to sit on.

I was immediately aware of lots of flies buzzing around me but tried to ignore them and not let anyone see they bothered me. I soon forgot about them!!

We were shown around the home by Allan. There were three tiny bedrooms with "a sort of" bed in each and three of the children slept on the one bed in each room. There was only a tattered piece of material hanging over the entrance to each room. Later a lunch of boiled potatoes and beans, which had been cooked by the twin girls, was brought into the sitting area, there was a bowl for each of us.

I was amazed as even when they have nothing, a meal is always provided when one visits their home.

Allan is the eldest of eight children and the only one with any education. At Vision school he had achieved highly in his S5 exams scoring 19 points, the highest of all the ACE students. Then unfortunately in his S6 year his Mother had died leaving a baby girl who was still being breast fed. His father is an alcoholic and not able to care for the family which left Allan in turmoil. Naturally he was not able to concentrate fully on his studies at that time and his grades on his S6 exams were not up to his previous standard. He could not think about going to a University at that time.

Some considerable time after his results had come out, he decided to ask ACE if they would give him his sponsors email address. Understanding the whole situation Allan had found himself in, his sponsor, a friend of mine in Scarborough, decided to support him at a college on an Electrical Engineering two years degree course. At the time of writing this he is nearing the end of the two years and is achieving very highly. His sponsor is so very happy she has been able to give this very personable young man a career.

CHAPTER 17

Rwanda and Home

The 29th June was to be my last day in Uganda on this visit. After breakfast my luggage was packed into the car and Boss was to drive Denis and myself to Kigali airport in Rwanda where I was to fly home from. It is only around 6 or 7 miles to the border between Uganda and Rwanda.

At the border Denis and I got out and went to one queue while Boss took the car to another. When it came to my turn to buy my Rwanda VISA, I had plenty of money in both Sterling and Ugandan money, but however we tried they would not take either, insisting on only USA dollars.

After lots of time trying to explain and getting nowhere, we went to find Boss to request he drive us back to Kisoro to a bank. In the meantime, Boss had been advised to use someone who was used to driving in Rwanda to drive us all while in the Rwandan countryside, because of their driving laws and keen police checks. So now with Boss sitting in the back of the car and Denis in the front with the new driver we had to go back to Kisoro, to a bank to exchange enough money into USA dollars to pay for the VISA. Denis went into the bank joined the queue, which was so long, to change the money. When he arrived back to us, he held the money in his hand. When our new driver saw it, he exclaimed it was too tattered and was sure the men at the border would complain and not take it. Denis had to go back into the bank, queue again and ask for newer notes to be given. All this of course took lots of time.

We drove back to the border, where again I had to join a long queue. While waiting for my turn two young white girls from the UK were trying to get back into Rwanda. They were Doctors working for six months in a local hospital. They had been visiting Uganda for a one-day visit. They were also being given an extremely hard time with their passports and visas.
Eventually I got to the two windows side by side, at one sat a Ugandan man and almost touching him sat a Rwandan man. The one took my dollars and handed them over to the other then I had to wait for a further 15 mins for my visa to be stamped and handed over to me.!!!! Now we could proceed to the Kigali airport.

What a beautiful scenic drive we had through the mountains. We arrived in Kigali and soon found the signs to the airport. At the airport the parking charges were very expensive so to save on costs Denis and myself were dropped off with my luggage.

I said my goodbye to Boss who had become a friend, an excellent driver, and nothing had been too much trouble for him. The two drivers then left the airport to go and wait in an area where there were no charges.
Denis and I then sat in an outside café in beautiful sunshine, drinking iced coffee. Sometime later it was time for us to say our goodbyes, both feeling very sad and

emotional, as we had planned that he would be given a VISA and would be flying back with me to the United Kingdom. However, on this occasion a VISA had been refused.

Denis walked away, not looking back, and I knew he was very upset not only the fact that he could not come to the UK but also not being able to fly in an aeroplane. At one point he had asked me if I could ask the pilot if he could just go and touch the aeroplane!! He had never been near an airport before, neither did he know what security we must go through.

CHAPTER 18

Marialuz and Nobua

I went through the usual procedure and eventually arrived in the seated waiting area. While sitting there a lady travelling on her own came and sat beside me. After a while we started chatting to each other. She asked me what I had been doing in Rwanda. I said I was just flying home from there.

I told her had been in Uganda to attend the Graduation in Kampala of a young man who had now graduated as a Doctor with a Bch of Medicine and Bch of Surgery. I told her that I had been his sponsor since meeting him in 2010 and had promised him that if ever he graduated, I would go to Uganda to see him graduate.

She was very interested in my story and at one point I told her I was thinking of writing a book about our first meeting and the consequences. She was a lady called Marialuz, from Washington in the USA. And she had been in Rwanda carrying out charity work on behalf of the International Monetary Fund. Before we moved to get on our aeroplanes she gave me her business card and said that if I sent her an e mail when I arrived home she was sure she and her husband would be able to give me a donation for Denis, "my boy". We then said goodbye as I

was called to go to my gate to catch my flight to Brussels, and then a connecting flight to Manchester.
Back home I was busy and at first misplaced the business card which Marialuz had given to me. However, a few weeks later I found it and decided to send her an e mail letter.

A few weeks later I received a lovely reply, saying she had been away on business but was delighted to receive my letter and she and her husband Nobuo would like to give Denis a donation to help with his living expenses while doing his Internship in the Lubaga hospital in Kampala.

We discussed how the money was going to get to Denis from the USA. She then told me that her husband worked for the World Bank and he was going to Uganda on business soon, she would give me the dates later when known. We decided that it would be best if Nobuo, who had said he would like to meet with Denis, took the money with him to hand over personally.
Marialuz also requested that she would like to have a live chat with me on the telephone from America.

We arranged a suitable time and date and spent a few minutes talking about our last meeting at which I had told her that I intended to write a book about how I had met Denis and what had happened since meeting him.

She gave me great encouragement and suggested that it could be a very good way of making money from the sales of the book in the future, to raise funds for the Victorious Medical Centre which Denis was setting up in one of the impoverished areas of south western Uganda.

Towards the end of February 2019 Nobuo arrived in Kampala on business. He contacted Denis and they arranged to meet for dinner the following evening at 7pm. Well, sometimes things do not always go to plan and this meeting was just one of those occasions.

During the afternoon Denis received a message from Nobuo telling him that his Mother who lives in Japan had had a massive heart attack and he must cancel their meeting to go to her. He was to fly to Japan on the next aeroplane that evening. Naturally Nobuo and Denis did not meet on that occasion.

I very thankfully heard from Marialuz sometime later that Nobuo's Mother had survived, but it would take a very long time for her to make a full recovery.

Marialuz and I continued to correspond with each other. Although Nobuo's Mother was still in hospital and seriously ill Nobuo arranged to go back to Uganda from the 7th to the 11th May 2019. He invited Denis to meet him for dinner one evening in the Serena Hotel where he was staying.

Later Denis told me that he had enjoyed a delicious buffet supper and felt that the two of them had spent a most interesting and informative evening together. Not only talking about Denis completing his Internship and setting up a small medical centre and the great need for financial help with it, but also Denis was able to give advice to Nobuo, who works for the World Bank, about what is needed to help the impoverished people and farmers in his mountainous area of Uganda .

It was sometime during that evening when Nobuo handed over $300 to Denis as a gift from Marialuz and himself, to help Denis with his living costs while completing his Internship.

I had five hours to wait in Brussels. So, I took my time and stretched my legs and slowly walked the long way to get to the gate for my final flight. Once in the area I stood around for a while. A gentleman came across to ask which flight I was waiting for.

He and his wife, who had gone to the ladies' room, had just arrived from the USA and were on their way to Manchester, then for a walking holiday in the lake district. He asked where I had come from and what had I been doing in Uganda, a lady on my own. I told him and when his wife a little later came to join us her husband explained what I had just told him.

The husband then said he was going for a little walk about and asked his wife to join him. She said' no' she was going to sit down beside me as she was so interested to hear all about my years of supporting and raising funds for this poverty-stricken young man from Uganda who was now a Doctor.

As her husband came back to join us, she said to him, "I am going to give Val something for this young man". She put her hand into her handbag and to my great surprise she gave me not just a couple of dollars BUT $60. I thanked her profusely and asked for her email address and told her I would tell Denis when I reached home. He later sent her a delightful thank you message.

These coincidences just seem to keep happening to me!

CHAPTER 19

An Unplanned Visit

I had been invited to give a talk to the Scalby Wives Club about ACE and my sponsoring a boy in Uganda and my visits to that country. One of the members called Doreen, had been so inspired and moved by how I was giving someone who has nothing, an education. She discussed it with her husband and then came to me and asked if I would inform Angela, Chairman of ACE that they would like to sponsor a child, preferably a girl.

At the start of the school year in 2015 Doreen began to sponsor a girl called Monic.

In early 2018 sadly, Doreen's husband Sydney died. Some months later Doreen, now living on her own, asked if I would take her with me to Uganda in the June to meet Monic, I said yes, and we began to make plans. Unfortunately, she developed health problems and was told she would have to have an operation. She was devastated at not being able to come with me!

I promised her that when she had fully recovered after her heart operation, I would take her to Uganda. Me, thinking it would be "at least" into the next year before that could happen!!

Shortly after my return from Uganda in June, Doreen called me with great delight to tell me she did not need to have a heart operation after all. Her cardiologist said she was free to fly. Immediately, she asked, when would we be able to go to Uganda.? Denis had been given his date to start his year of Internship which was in early October 2018. I knew he would not be free to be our guide until the following Easter. Doreen exclaimed, 'Oh, can't we go before then!'

Denis and I had a long discussion and decided that the only other time we could be together would be just before he started his Internship, a decision was made. Doreen was ecstatic with excitement that she was going to AFRICA.

Together Denis and I planned our itinerary. He contacted Boss to be our driver again and hired his car, he booked all our accommodation including a night in the Queen Elizabeth National Park and a night in a lodge in the Impenetrable Forest National park, so that Doreen could track and see the Gorillas. Doreen and I booked our flights from 29th September until 11th October 2018.

CHAPTER 20

Doreen's visit

At 1.15am on 29th September my daughter Jane once again drove me and this time Doreen all the way to Manchester airport, dropped us off and immediately drove back home.

Denis's sister Moreen had been studying for two years on a tailoring course, but she did not possess a sewing machine, which she would need to start a small business once she completed the course. I decided I would give her mine as I rarely used it.

Carrying a Singer sewing machine with a clip over case which in all weighed 11 kg. became quite a struggle and problem for me as I took it as my hand luggage. I had packed it beautifully wrapped in strong black plastic with just the handle out for me to carry it by, and securely fastened with lots of strong insulating tape.

We hit the first problem at Manchester airport when I was asked to take off all the plastic covering, being informed that the contents would not show on the x ray machine. Having gone through the machine successfully I was told I could repack it, but they had nothing I could use. Anyway, what was I carrying a sewing machine for? Luckily for me a very kind Indian man came to my rescue and told them he fully understood as he had seen lots of people take them out to India for the poor people there. He found more plastic and Sellotape and helped me to secure it to carry again.

For the whole journey I found it a real struggle to carry, it seemed miles to the gates, up many stairs and along long slopes. I was surprised as the only help I received on the whole journey was from two separate black ladies. Not a man in sight!!! Was I delighted to hand it over to Denis as soon as we met!

Denis, right, carrying the Sewing Machine, me, centre, and Boss, our driver, left, carrying my luggage.

The outcome of this small gesture is, that Moreen set up a tiny business in a unit she rented in a market area as she has no electricity in her home. I have been told since that she was given a contract to go to a school and make all the uniforms for the children at that school. Other school contracts have followed. Now she works full time and she has made enough money for her husband to build a much larger house of bricks for them to live in.

It is incredible what a difference one small gift can make! However, I will never be persuaded to carry a sewing machine to Uganda again!

I had decided to exit the flight in Kigali, Rwanda, as we were starting our visit from Kisoro which is just over the border from Rwanda. It took us such a long time to get through customs control, collect our luggage and walk out to arrivals that Boss said to Denis that we must not be on the flight. Fortunately, I had TEXT Denis from Brussels and told him we had boarded the flight. Denis and I were so excited to be meeting each other again so soon after my visit in June.

Unfortunately, with us being so late getting through customs the nearest border crossing into Uganda had closed for the night at 9 pm. We had no choice but to go the long way around to the next crossing at Gatuna and then through Kabale. This made our journey to Kisoro a very long one. We eventually arrived at the Countryside Guest House around 1.30 am. Even though the Manager Francis had been in bed he greeted us very warmly and insisted on giving us food and hot drinks before we could retire to our room and beds.

The next morning even as we were having our breakfast Juliet and Mandela turned up to greet me. News travels fast in Uganda.!! I had decided that I would take Doreen on a leisurely stroll through the town and up to a fantastic view of Kisoro from the top of a long hill. We were joined on this walk not only by Denis and Boss but also Mandela and David, the ACE Rep, in Uganda. I was reminiscing but also having the pleasure of showing my friend the amazing views around Kisoro. That afternoon we drove to Ruhija to the Rushaga gorilla Lodge where we were going to spend the night, to be very early up the following morning for Doreen to trek to see the Gorillas.
One of Denis's brothers called Onesmus works as a Ranger in the Bwindi Impenetrable Forest National Park and is involved in the Gorilla tracking. This was very fortunate for Doreen, as it was through him that Denis had been able to get the $600 permit which Doreen paid, to enable her to track and see the Gorillas at such short notice.

Doreen came back mid-afternoon looking so exhausted. She had to be carried the last hundred or so yards by the porters to enable her to see the wonderful Busingye family of gorillas. While Doreen was on the trek Denis and I relaxed in comfortable seats in the garden with spectacular views of the Impenetrable range of mountains before us.

After a late lunch in this beautiful Lodge we packed and departed to drive to see the government IV clinic which Dr Denis had been working in voluntary for some months until our arrival.

We were shown over the whole clinic. We were both appalled at the conditions inside. Apart from the operating theatre everywhere was dirty. Denis told us there was a cleaning person, but he/she hardly ever turned up. He told us that the generator was broken, and no one came to repair it, so when there was no electricity, which happens often, no operations could be performed. There was no ambulance.

If a pregnant lady was needing a caesarean section, she had to be put on a motorbike and sent to Kisoro hospital miles away. The roads are all volcanic rocks and mud. Often the mother or the baby died on the way.

The resident doctor paid by the government had gone to work in his private clinic for the duration of Dr Denis's time there. Seeing the conditions in this clinic was extremely upsetting. Later we all discussed it and I again felt very strongly that it would be good if we could raise funds to set up a model health centre for Denis to be a director of and Doctor in charge after he had completed his Internship.

After seeing this clinic, we drove back to the Countryside Guest house in Kisoro for dinner and two further night's stay.

Tuesday was to be a big day for Doreen for she was going to meet the young girl Monic she had been sponsoring for over four years.

We had made an appointment to visit Standard school some days before. All the ACE students had been moved to this school from Vision the previous year.

Monic was nervously waiting to be introduced to her sponsor. We left the two of them to have a little time together. The headmaster Elisa and one of his staff showed us all around the school which needs a lot of modernization. Monic is an orphan and has been living with her grandparents also her two sisters ever since their parents died. They had invited us to their home for lunch as they naturally wanted to meet Doreen.

The grandparents could both speak English which was so pleasing to be able to converse with them. At one-point Denis whispered to me that this home was in much better condition than his parents' home, these people were not as poor as many around them. I had noticed and agreed with him.

Later back in Kisoro we called in at Countryside for we "white (Masungu)) ladies" to use our modern toilets before taking Monic and Juliet with us for English afternoon tea in The Coffee Pot tea rooms. Monic was then taken back to her school. I know it had been a very rewarding and successful day for Doreen and Monic.

Another journey for us all the next day when we travelled from Kisoro through the national parks and their stunning scenery. Now very familiar for me but the first time for Doreen. Each time I am driven through them I hope to see the forest elephants crossing the road, but the nearest I have ever been to see them was, once we saw fresh dung droppings!! I live in hope!

Butaogota, and The Bwindi Forest Cottages guest house was our destination where I had stayed on my visit earlier in the year. We were greeted very warmly and after settling in and relaxing we were joined by two of Denis's brothers who had dinner with us.

The whole of the next day we spent at the home of Denis's parents. Moreen was there and so excited to unpack and see her sewing machine. We could not demonstrate it as there was no electricity in the home. Thankfully I had taken a detailed Singer Sewing machine instruction booklet.

Doreen was introduced to everyone and shown around the land. She was fascinated to watch one of the brothers standing in a hollowed-out tree trunk and treading on bananas in the process of turning them into alcohol. We were also given the usual welcome of singing and dancing by the children in the nearby school, of course they made sure we joined in the dancing.

We departed Butogota on the Saturday early and travelled to the Queen Elizabeth National Park arriving at 1pm. Outside our rooms we were greeted by a family of warthogs busy eating the grass. We ate lunch sitting outside overlooking the Kazinga channel and on the banks, we could see a herd of Elephants and also Hippopotamus, and Meerkats where all around us.

Denis had booked a boat ride for us at 3pm.I could see he was rather nervous at getting on the boat but eventually I called to him and he boarded at the last minute. Much later he told me he had never been on a boat as he did not like deep water. It took him a while to relax but eventually he enjoyed it as much as we did. I never realised until then that many Ugandans have never been into any of their own national parks or seen elephants, lions, crocodiles or giraffes etc, as they cannot afford the costs. Our cruise lasted 2½ hours.

The following morning, we were up very early and at 6.30 am we were ready for our Game Drive. Denis and Boss were also invited to join us, neither had been on a game drive before. We were extremely lucky to see a lonesome lion soon after we set off. Great excitement for me as I had not seen a lion in the park on my previous visit. We had an excellent guide and we saw every species of animal that lives in the QENP. A real bonus, we were just about at the end of our drive when we came across a large family of elephants by the roadside drinking, and the baby ones playing in a pool of water. We stopped to watch them for ages and were able to take lots of video as well as pictures.

We arrived back at base at 11am.

I had arranged to meet Allan for lunch that day. He was still studying at college in Fort Portal. He travelled by bus and we had arranged to meet him on the outskirts of the QENP. He was waiting for us. We then drove to the Tempo Lodge which overlooks a beautiful stretch of water. After greetings and cool drinks, we each ordered an Avocado salad for lunch. It was a real pleasure to meet Allan again and I was able to give him gifts which his sponsor Nahar had given me to take for him. After lunch we said our goodbyes to Allan and he caught another bus back to Fort Portal.

At 1.30pm we left the area and Boss drove us to Ishaka where we were to spend the night in the Crane Hotel. I could not believe that we were going to be staying overnight in the hotel where so many years before, in 2011 I had taken Denis, Ojok and Mandella for dinner on 2 consecutive evenings for dinner.
At the time it was the smartest hotel each of them had ever eaten in!!

Boss by this time had become one of "The Fab Four" and his home was in Ishaka. When he knew we would be staying the night in the town he had messaged his wife who unfortunately was working so she could not meet us. Not to be beaten he then contacted his Mother and asked her to prepare a meal for us that evening. Again, no effort was spared, and we enjoyed a delicious meal in her home. We were introduced to Boss's Mother, a delightful lady, and other members of the family. After dropping us off at the Crane Hotel Boss was able to go to his own home and spend the night with his wife and young son.

On the Monday we were up and on the road by 6 am as we had a very long journey ahead. We travelled via Mbarara and, Masaka and eventually reached our destination in Kampala at 2 pm. We were to stay once again in the colonial luxury house in which Denis's family and I had stayed in the June. Doreen was amazed and delighted to be staying in this lovely home which I had previously told her about.

The staff greeted us like family and could not do enough for us during our time there. After the long journey we had a light lunch together.
Later Doreen and I relaxed while Boss and Denis went off at 3 pm into the city to exchange some British money into Ugs. Saying as they left 'We won't be long'.! We became very anxious when they still had not returned by 7pm. Convinced they must have had an accident!! However, they had been stuck in Kampala's horrendous traffic, which must be experienced to be believed. They eventually arrived back at 7.30pm. What a relief!!

Denis and Boss then cooked a hot meal for us all. We had boiled bananas cooked in their skins, their skins taken off at the table just before eating, boiled rice, avocados and groundnut sauce. Followed by fresh juicy pineapple for dessert.

CHAPTER 21

Mobile Phone

During our journey to Kampala Denis received a telephone message asking if one of us who had slept in the 'zebra' bedroom had lost a mobile phone, as one had been found in a pink cover, under a pillow. It was mine!! During the night I use it as a clock.

Boss then called his wife and asked her to go and pick it up from the hotel, and to put it on a bus to Kampala. Someone he knew would pick it up at the end of the journey. I could not believe this would work.! However, the next day during the afternoon we were out in the car in the middle of Kampala and Boss received a message telling him a friend/acquaintance now had my mobile and he was bringing it to Boss on a motorbike. They arranged a place to meet and after a short while Boss pulled the car in to the roadside and stopped. Suddenly in the distance a motorbike appeared, it came over to the car and handed the mobile over to us. To me the most amazing thing was that the mobile wasn't even wrapped in anything. It was just still with its pink covering showing. No name or anything on it to say where or who it had to be delivered to. It had been returned to me after an overnight journey on a bus, I was astounded!! I'm quite sure that would not have happened in England!!

CHAPTER 22

Kampala, our Last Day

Our last full day in Kampala was on Denis's 27th birthday so we went out for a celebration lunch to a special Gym where the dining area overlooked a swimming pool. Unfortunately, the setting was rather spoiled for us. We arrived as a terrific thunderstorm raged around us, the rain continued to pour down throughout the meal.

It had been a long-held wish for Denis, that one year the two of us would spend his birthday together. That wish had now been granted.

Back in the luxurious home we completed our packing. We set off at 7.30 pm for Entebbe airport to catch our flight due to depart at 10.50 pm. Usually a journey of about 1 hour. Due to the horrendous traffic in Kampala for the whole journey, we only arrived at the airport 5 minutes before the gate for our flight closed. A very close shave!!

The rest of our journey home was uneventful.

CHAPTER 23

Internship

The next day Dr Denis started his Internship in the Lubaga private hospital, Kampala. He had found a very small but empty room to rent for the year. This was directly across the road from the main entrance to the hospital. Landlords could demand and receive high rents for their accommodation near the hospital. Because for Interns who had to work at all hours of the day and night, they needed to be very near. So again, through sponsorship and fund raising, money was provided for Denis to buy a bed and other necessary items for his room. Also, for all his food and personal living expenses. Throughout their year as an intern these doctors do not receive any pay.

This is what Denis wrote about his year of INTERNSHIP:

Medical internship in Uganda is another one-year training one gets after 5 ½ years of study in a medical school, done in only referral hospitals of the country, under supervision of consultants in different disciplines of medicine, upon which successful completion awards you two things.

1 - Full registration as a medical practitioner.
2 - Annual practicing licence.

I started my internship in October 2018 from Lubaga hospital, Kampala, Uganda and finished in October 2019. It was such a nice experience to be is such an advanced hospital setting, in a city and yet I had entirely grown up and studied in a village!!

I had to interact with classy people, walk in the city, eat from posh hotels, work from posh clinical rooms/consultation rooms. Most importantly was everything is done in a modern way.

This made me change my career from obstetrics and gynaecology to surgery. By the time I finished medical school, I loved being a gynaecologist in the future, but on reaching Lubaga hospital, I changed my mind. .I started assisting in laparoscopic surgeries for example that I loved and got interested in so much. I also did several operations including, caesarean section, herniorrhaphy, appendicectomy, uterine evacuation, chest tube insertions, abdominal paracentesis, and so on and so forth. Because I was quite confident and eager to learn. Generally, my stay in Lubaga hospital was the best because I learnt lots of things in all disciplines.

October 27th, 2019 was the day when Denis had completed all his basic training and become a fully registered medical practitioner, with an Annual practicing license. After spending a few days holiday with me as I was once again in Uganda, Denis went straight to Butogota to be the director and doctor in charge of the Victorious Medical Centre, where he is presently working full time. He is already saving the lives of people in his own impoverished area of Uganda. After two years 'practice' he plans to go and study for his Masters.

CHAPTER   24

Helping in the 3rd World

After my two daughters reached their late teens and left home, I often had the feeling that I would like to go to an African country to help impoverished people in some useful way. However, I told myself that I would not be useful to anyone as I had no professional training which I thought would be needed, perhaps in the nursing or teaching profession. At that time, I had not realised that I could have helped in an orphanage or taught handicrafts such as dressmaking, knitting, crocheting, etc.

It was on a weekend visit while staying with some friends in Essex, that I went to their Sunday morning church service and while socialising after, I expressed my thoughts and feelings to one of the parishioners, a senior member of that church. She asked if she could pray for me. She held her hands just above my head and prayed for me to be given guidance. After some time had passed, I thought no more about this incident.

It was only after spending my holiday with my sister in Uganda, and meeting with Denis and later becoming his sponsor, that I realized my desire to help the under privileged people in Africa had been granted.

I had retired and although I enjoy working in my garden, have a good social life and various voluntary jobs, I strongly felt I needed a new purpose in my life.

My four delightful grandchildren were growing up and beginning to think more about being on their computers than playing games with or going on the beach with Grandma.

I truly feel that January 2010 was a very appropriate time for Denis, my unofficial Ugandan Grandson, now Dr Musasizi Denis, Bachelor of Medicine and Bachelor of Surgery, to come into my life.

God works in wonderous ways!!

Printed in Great Britain
by Amazon